## LITTLE

# In Elizabethan Times

Fiona MacDonald

Kingfisher

# Contents

# Elizabeth I

Queen Elizabeth I ruled England between 1558 and 1603. When she first came to the throne, many people thought that a woman would not be able to govern the country. However, Elizabeth soon proved them wrong. She was wise, clever and brave, and became one of the most popular rulers who ever lived.

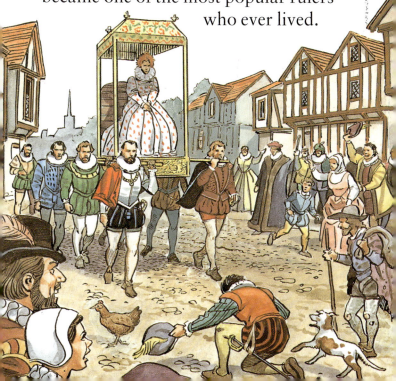

# A wise ruler

Elizabeth's father, King Henry VIII died in 1547. England was then ruled by Elizabeth's young brother, Edward, and then by her sister, Mary. These three made many enemies, both at home and abroad. Elizabeth worked hard to bring peace, and to defend England from invaders.

Elizabeth wisely asked Parliament for advice, and chose trustworthy councillors to help her rule the country.

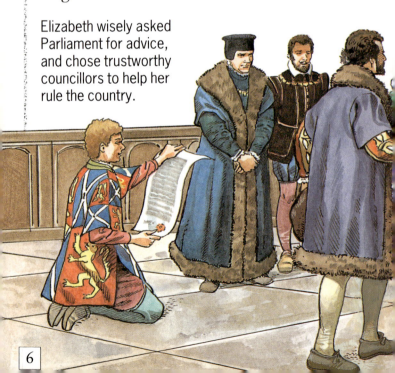

## ELIZABETH'S RIVAL

Mary, Queen of Scots
was Elizabeth's cousin.
She plotted to replace
Elizabeth as queen,
but her plans failed
and she was finally
beheaded for treason.

# Royal fashions

Elizabeth was very proud of her appearance, especially her white skin, beautiful hands and curly red hair. She loved perfume, make-up and splendid clothes. Like other wealthy women of the day, she wore gowns of rich velvet, fine linen and shimmering silk, trimmed with jewels, lace and fur.

Rich men and boys wore embroidered jackets, fur-lined robes, and short padded trousers called breeches.

Rich women and girls wore dresses with tight bodices. Their wide skirts were stiffened by hoops and padding, and they wore lace ruffs around their necks.

# MAKE A COURTIER'S HAT

You will need a large piece of material, some card, scissors and glue to make this Elizabethan hat.

**1** Cut a rim from card to fit comfortably around your head.
**2** Using the card rim as a guide, draw an identical rim on the material. Cut it out, and glue it to one side of the card rim.

**3** Cut out a large circle from the rest of the material (about 60 cm in diameter).
**4** Put the rim of card on top of the large circle, and pull the material through until the edges are just below it.

**5** Glue the gathered edges to the card. Cut a feather and a jewel from some more card, and sew or glue it to the side.

# Everyday clothes

Ordinary working people could not afford fine gowns and jackets. Their clothes had to be comfortable to work in, cheap to make, and strong enough to last for many years.

Clothes were sewn at home, from rough linen and hard-wearing wool. In cold weather, men, women and children wore many different layers in order to keep themselves warm.

## HAND-MADE CLOTHES

Women spun thread from woollen fleece. They then sold it to craftsmen, who wove it into cloth. Everything had to be done by hand, as there were no machines to help.

Left to right: a market trader, a schoolboy with a wooden hoop, a pedlar, a flower-seller, a vegetable-picker and her daughter, a farm worker (a harvester), and an old man.

# Food and drink

Most Elizabethan people ate simple meals, such as bread, cheese and soup, washed down with weak beer.

Richer people could afford costlier food, including luxuries from overseas. At great feasts, they enjoyed special dishes such as boiled boar's head, or salads decorated with flowers.

# GINGER BISCUITS

The Elizabethans enjoyed the flavour of ginger. To make these biscuits, you'll need 100 g butter, 100 g sugar, 200 g plain flour, 1 egg and 1 tsp powdered ginger.

**1** Heat the oven to gas mark 4 (180°C).
**2** Beat the butter and sugar together, until they're light and fluffy.
**3** Beat the egg, then add it to the mixture.
**4** Add the ginger and flour, and mix it all into a dough.

**5** Roll the dough out on a floured surface, until it's about 5 mm thick. Press out biscuit shapes with a cutter.

**6** Ask an adult to bake the biscuits for 15–20 minutes, or until they're pale brown. Then leave to cool on a wire tray.

# Life in the town

**E**lizabethan towns may have been dirty, smelly and noisy, but they were busy and exciting, too! There was always something interesting to look at – maybe a dancing bear, a juggler, or an acrobat. The streets were full of people selling goods, passing on gossip, or running errands.

### KEY TO STREET

1. Water carrier
2. Juggler on stilts
3. Dancing bear
4. Musician
5. Dirty water and sewage
6. Thief in pillory
7. Servant taking beer to an inn
8. Street trader

Petty criminals were locked in the pillory, where people jeered and threw rotten fruit at them.

# The first theatres

For hundreds of years, actors had performed wherever they could find the space – on street corners, village greens, or in the yards of inns. Then, during the 1500s, people began to build England's first real theatres. They had a proper stage, so that everyone could see the play. All kinds of people visited the theatres every week.

William Shakespeare was a very successful actor and playwright. His 37 plays, which were performed in the new theatres, are still hugely popular with audiences all over the world today.

## KEY TO GLOBE

① Covered seats, for rich people.
② Way in
③ Standing room ('the pit') for poor people. They often threw fruit at the actors on the stage!
④ Stage
⑤ Trap door, for 'magic' appearances.
⑥ Actors' entrances.
⑦ Stair turret

The Globe theatre was built in London in 1599. Many great Elizabethan actors performed here, including Shakespeare.

All the female parts were played by young men or boys. Women and girls were not allowed to perform in Elizabethan theatres.

# In a great house

The families of noblemen or rich merchants lived in splendid houses, surrounded by a private park and gardens. The houses had many rooms, decorated with dark wooden panelling, family portraits, and rich tapestries.

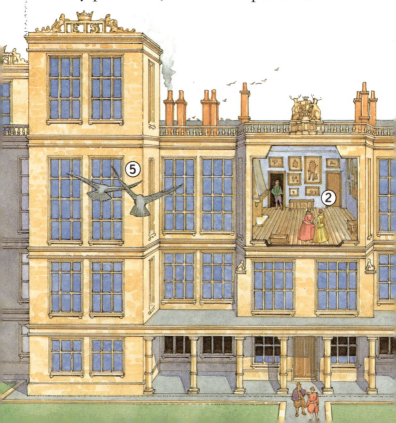

A big house needed dozens of different servants to run it, and to care for the family who lived in it. There were cooks, grooms, maintenance men, butlers, gardeners, ladies' maids, nurse-maids, messengers, and cleaners.

KEY TO HOUSE

① Bedchamber
② Upper gallery
③ Formal gardens, with many paths and flowerbeds bordered by hedges
④ Kitchen
⑤ Brick walls (a new idea!)

# Magic and medicine

Although there were doctors in most towns, their fees were expensive, and their treatments could sometimes be terrifying! Many men and women preferred to put their trust in old-fashioned herbal potions, which were brewed at home. Others relied on magic, or lucky charms.

Doctors didn't realise that germs could kill. Many soldiers died because their wounds became infected.

Elizabethan people believed that 'good' magic could cure diseases, but 'bad' magic caused harm. Many old women were accused of being witches, and were put to death.

Women made beauty aids and medicine from plants and flowers. Great country houses had a still-room, where all kinds of lotions and potions were prepared.

The medicines often worked. Many people still prefer to use herbal medicine today.

# Life in the country

In Elizabethan England, most people lived in villages in the country. The villagers worked very hard growing crops, rearing animals, and making the tools they needed to farm the land. Most of them rented their plots from rich land owners. They also had to earn money to pay the rent on their cottages, and to pay local taxes.

**TIME OFF**

On May Day, at Midsummer and during Christmas, the hard-working villagers took a break and made merry. They ate, drank, danced, and went to fairs.

The villagers were especially busy during the harvest. The crops had to be gathered as soon as they were ripe – if the grain was allowed to become wet and mouldy, everyone would starve during the winter months.

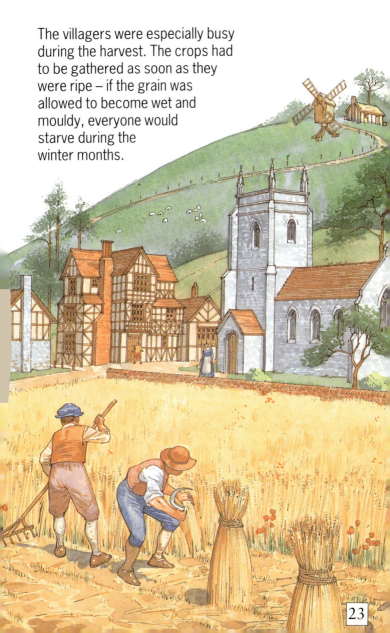

# Going to school

At the age of seven, rich boys were sent to grammar schools. Lessons began early in the morning, and lasted all day long. The teacher was very strict, and boys who made mistakes were punished severely.

The children from ordinary families did not go to school. They stayed home with their parents, helping with the work and learning the family trade.

Rich girls were taught at home by their mothers. They learnt reading, writing, and all the skills needed to run a great house.

At school, the boys sat on long benches called 'forms'. They had to learn long passages of text by heart.

Whoever got top marks was moved to sit at the 'top of the form', but those who did badly were beaten with a bundle of twigs, called a birch.

# Sea dogs

The Elizabethan 'sea dogs' were bold, ruthless sailors who explored new routes all around the world. During their journeys, they risked storms, shipwrecks and deadly disease. They were rewarded with vast fortunes, and won the favour of the queen.

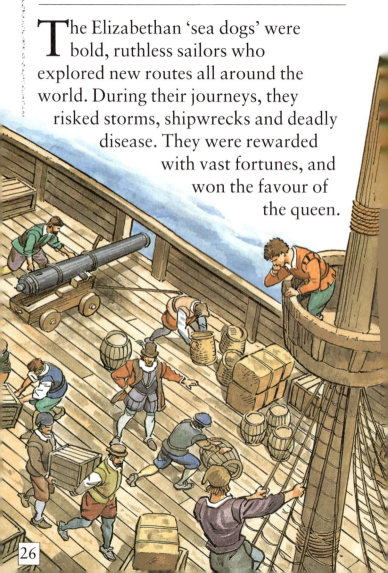

# FOOD FROM THE AMERICAS

Potatoes were first brought to England from South America in Elizabethan times.

Tobacco leaves were brought back from Virginia, in North America.

Peppers and hot, spicy chillis came from the Aztec lands, in Mexico.

Cacao beans also came from Mexico. They were used to make cocoa.

Elizabeth encouraged trade and exploration by lending money for the voyages. In return, she expected a share in any goods or treasure!

# The Armada

England and Spain were bitter rivals. Elizabeth encouraged her sailors to attack Spanish ships, and in return King Philip of Spain sent his fleet of warships to invade England. This fleet was called the 'Armada'.

The Spanish sailors were not used to the stormy seas around England, and many of their ships were wrecked. The Armada was defeated, and Elizabeth won a great victory.

## FRANCIS DRAKE

Sir Francis Drake was an explorer, a sea-captain, and a great favourite of the queen. In 1588, Drake led the English fleet to victory against the Spanish Armada.

# Index